BONES IN THEIR WINGS

HAGIOS
PRESS

BONES IN THEIR WINGS

~ ghazals ~

LORNA CROZIER

National Library of Canada
Cataloguing in Publication Data

Crozier, Lorna, 1948 –
 Bones in their wings : ghazals / Lorna Crozier.

 Includes bibliographical references.
 ISBN 0-9682256-6-7

 1. Ghazals. I. Title.
PS8555.R72B66 2003   C811'.54   C2003-911099-0

Printed and bound in Canada
Second printing: Spring 2004

The publishers gratefully acknowledge the assistance of the Saskatchewan Arts Board.

HAGIOS PRESS
Box 33024 Cathedral PO
Regina SK S4T 7X2

ACKNOWLEDGEMENTS

Thanks to Patrick, my best reader and ghazal mentor; to Paul Wilson for his fine eye and ear in editing this collection; to the Saskatchewan Artists and Writers Colonies for providing me with such a beautiful, sparse writing space; and to Shannon Bailey, Eve Joseph, Brad Cran, and Billeh Nickerson, who have continued the ghazal dialogue with me long after they ceased to be students. And my gratitude to Hagios for their immediate and enthusiastic response to these poems.

Special thanks to Coleman Barks for permission to use an excerpt from *The Essential Rumi* as the epigraph for this book. And to Anansi Press for their permission to use, within the afterword, excerpts from *Stilt Jack*, which is part of the collection *I Dream Myself Into Being: Collected Poems* by John Thompson.

CONTENTS

I am so small I can barely be seen.
How can this great love be inside me?

Look at your eyes. They are small,
but they see enormous things.

— Rumi
Translated by Coleman Barks

For Patrick, whom I now call *husband*,
and for Phyllis N. and all her love.

Do the birds know in their wings
they have bones? And me with no feathers.

Love is all flesh and then it's not.
A fossil with the soft tissue gone.

I've broken all the wishbones
you were drying on the windowsill.

Done with beauty, this week's
unexpected snow turns to slush.

A wish, a foretelling. Most days
it's the weather gets me out of bed.

My Tai Chi master has Parkinson's,
a slight shudder in the stillest pose.

To the cat, every bird's a Lazarus.
A flick of his paw — it stutters and flies.

Though I gave you ancient *I Ching* coins
you insist on new pennies.

Roast another chicken. I'll read
the gizard and its tiny stones.

Scorpions eat their young. A genetic
winnowing. The slowest go first.

Danger. No blame in this,
six in the third place means.

The wild leaps into the autumn maple,
blood on its mind.

A mourning dove grieves anywhere its heart
can rise to: stiltjack, tree top, Jacob's ladder.

Once a singer, he puts two fingers
over the hole in his throat so he can speak.

Wind won't chatter. It mouths the words
it lifts from grass to golden aspen.

Incarnadine. If the cardinal did not exist,
you'd fashion him from fire.

That small dark O where the tumour was
cut out? He makes me look inside.

Night heron. Is she the same
as day's long-legged strider?

Raked in grass, black mushrooms
leave a printer's smear of ink.

Rats and slugs hollow out the fallen
apples. Eat the goodness and the rot.

Varied Thrush, Russet-Sided Towhee.
Throw in a beautiful bird or two!

The moon floating in the pond:
water's mind lit up with wonder.

This weary fly has flown so far
I can see right through its wings.

It was my father who shot the neighbours'
dogs or horses or whatever.

The bullet hit my heart — O death —
but I couldn't leave my body.

Some doors will not close.
The cellar's dank breath at your back.

Cancer in the dog's gut, a broken fetlock.
To kill out of kindness — that's the worst.

The prairie sky is twin to the ocean:
the same restlessness, the blue unfolding.

Once, the dead drank with the living,
thin lips gripping the same cup.

He washes my eyes with fennel tea
and the redness goes away.

The stones around the pond come from
everywhere. Get rained on and turn blue.

In Wales my grandpa sang to horses;
then willow-whipped his children.

Iron in the water of the well,
old trout at the bottom chewing nails.

To fence the borders with barbed wire,
how much anger does it take?

If snow had fallen, there'd be more
light here, there'd be forgiveness.

Stories from the Old Country,
meanness too.

I'm too cheeky for Tai Chi.
I lack the finer graces. What gets lost?

The only way to live the moment:
tree frog singing in winter's grip.

Before the change, three days.
After the change, three days.

Goldfish small and bright as . . .
temple bells in freezing water?

To be as cold and clear
as that. And have no need to ring.

This is the only place you'll find
the name Lady Junco.

If someone is not as he should be,
he has misfortune.

To be, do be, doo. Hamlet scatting.
Your feet's too big.

A February score: snowdrops, forty-three
under the sycamore; hyacinth, two.

My body's unilingual. It's forgotten
snow and its dozen words for wonder.

Voiceless. Wounded. Out of touch.
Are there angels that inhabit longing?

Between the ice and the water running
a river is neither. Neither are you.

Full of lust I buy the title:
An Inordinate Fondness for Beetles.

So many possibilities: spoons,
orchids, bee-keeping, garlic, you.

The work goes slowly here;
the wind is fasting.

Three things keep me sane.
Two of them, four-legged.

Was it you who left the tabby's ashes
in the blue bowl by my door?

I love my cats more than I care to say.
Say it anyway. Double dare you.

Hoarfrost on the telephone wires:
it's the old ones talking.

Hand on the tamarack —
startled, the tree touches back.

At birth with honey my mother drew
a third eye on my tongue.

Jackrabbit! May these *shers*
have your strong back legs.

A grasshopper's tick, tick, tick.
What to do with its savvy, sad reminder?

For every grass blade there's a singer.
That's what happens when rain is rare.

Confabulation. Crows and chickadees.
A nuthatch too! Who gets the suet first?

That old horse once won all the races.
They called him Lucky though he'd run out.

Bursitis, arthritis, tendonitis.
A burnt-out bulb has a rattle.

Nine in the second place means:
A one-eyed man is able to see.

Here's stuff for the recycling box:
olive jar, egg carton, dead light.

How sweet the art of seeing!
For balance and good measure I lick salt.

O beggar lover, I would fill your hands
with gladness if you didn't need bread.

Chapped lips, squint lines. Sandpaper Wind,
how you bring out the grain, wear me down.

All the animals are sleeping,
their breath, my breath, the night easing in.

Here is your water and your watering place.
If your gods won't listen, start to dance!

A friend wakes up and is my enemy. Rather
Ovid's women turning into stars and trees.

Solace: a bench beneath the branches.
Step by step, five couplets make a path.

I look back over my shoulder
to see where I'm not going.

Old prayer: I'll say it anyway,
my soul, my Lord, to keep.

No worse, there is none. These words
the Jesuit poet willed to fire.

Lost in the mountains would I be
laughing with Wang Wei?

No blame in this. Now hot, now cold,
and you without a jacket.

Joyce in *Ulysses: It was a nun,
they say, invented barbed wire.*

Six at the beginning means:
He brings help with the strength of horses.

The old truck that once hauled hay
carries the Rodeo Queens in the Osoyoos Parade.

O clumsy one — simply put — begin
and end every movement with this.

I've learned to bow with my hands
clasped in the proper manner.

God's cadillac, God's palomino.
Now I'm in the driver's seat!

What's to choose? Skating on green ice
when thaw begins, the river running.

The Shushartie River is home
to black bear and salmon.

Before he stepped into the noose
the outlaw said, *Such is life*.

We may have to move
because we can't raise chickens.

Imitate the rain when you feel lonely.
The grass when you fear joy.

Up close or distant, not every eye
can hold a desert. Trees, the absence of.

Saskatchewan.
Chew on that one, said the wind.

Qu Ru paints a picture on a grain
of rice, a poem on a single hair.

Small unlikely wonders! The feet of flies —
black stitches in a spider's web.

Hasidic wisdom says that God
made the world to tell him stories.

The narrative of trees and beetles,
the dénouement of worms.

I'd like a Tennessee Walking Horse
just to walk with me.

Stay awake all day. Something's
moving past you with the speed of life.

The cat's tongue lapping water:
memory starts with such a sound.

Even my earlobes are wrinkled,
and look! The inside of my wrists.

A lamp held under paper, the past
shines through the sentence.

Was, was, *wasps*. Small dangerous
machines for making parchment.

A god walks among the pots and pans.
Sometimes you see his face, reflected.

The work goes slowly. My latest poems,
the grey ones, written on my hair.

Split-ends. Enjambment.
The *rimas dissolutus* of getting old.

Use your knots for nets
if you can't untie them.

Red flush of spawning pickerel,
a spondee's muscled gleam.

My bones are a gift from the river stones.
Are there gods who need no slaking?

Stand in the wrong place.
Wade to your waist in wonder.

Water makes a bed for you,
white rushes spread beneath.

There are angels in the apple tree,
polishing the winter apples.

Cold on the teeth. The bare legs
of shadows swish across the lawn.

Why is it still winter in these lines of birds
and flowers? Fritillaria. Plover.

A crow exploded on the power line.
Reading the *Díwán* in the dark.

My wrist refuses to hold the hours.
No praise in this. No blame.

In the drowned field, five swans swim
among the floating pumpkins.

Such beauty in what won't be gathered,
the season finely out of tune.

Stuff a yellow shirt around the window
to stop the wind. Still, the heart turns cold.

Not the other way around,
stars were made in snow's likeness.

Frost ferns on the window panes.
It's your breath that lets you see!

Only rain wants inside. Snow stays
in the dark where it can shine.

So many griefs you've gathered,
every pocket has a hole.

The prairie sky at noon looks nowhere
in particular. I avert my gaze.

Take your glass eye out and clean it.
A little spit will do.

"Carry Tiger To Mountain."
My feet stumble on that step —

The quartz from Rose Spit turns diamond
when I lick it. O, lapidary tongue!

That artificial leg the boy outgrew?
His mother used it for a planter.

Montaigne said, *See how many ends
this stick has?* Words as well.

Petunias, pansies and lobelia
started walking. With a limp.

The *ah* in *pond*: water praising
the shape your shovel dug.

Memory casts a shadow —
that must mean the mind's all light.

She said she'd marry me if I changed
my name to Moon and blew up the pipeline.

All my stories end in snow.
Rain's pen leaks and keeps on writing.

Bad luck is a hole in your gumboot,
a lumpy mend, mothbelly full of wool.

The hum's from the highway. No, it's under
my feet — the earth's deep, unborn-again choir.

At eighty-one, my prairie mother grins —
her first time under an umbrella!

Rumi says parched lips
are a message from the water.

Mr. Moon,
I want to hear from you.

No eyelid. The pond sees everything without
a blink. Fish, dragonfly, fish! fish! Sun.

The daffodil pickers are back.
A field of turbans and yellow slickers.

The rice fields sway with music.
Why no song for gathering flowers?

The word *pond* goes deep.
The sound of water, thinking.

The red-winged blackbird trills,
the duck does not.

I light a daffodil to read by
till I fall asleep.

Seven words for wisdom:
not one of them will do.

Think of the earth as water
and you can row across the furrows.

Memory needs a place to go.
How deep are your pockets?

In the old poet's garden
there's always a beetle to name.

Ambrosia. Spruce Engraver.
Flower Longhorn. Potato Bug.

The Russian mare chews open the gate,
steps aside for me to walk through.

A raven's sounds — two hundred discernable
to our instruments of measure.

O pain,
O Deuteronomy!

I held a blind crow in my hand —
it looked right at me.

In my mother's kitchen, unattended,
bread dough devours the bowl.

These tears come from cold
not sadness, but I could cry for you.

In the feeder, snowfall on a finch's beak.
How beautiful that drift!

Rain, sleet, snow, and something
we've no name for.

That slow falling may simply be
morning's many seeds of light.

In the photo the blue-eyed kitten
is smaller than a jar of sweet peas.

With thin wet fingers, rain touch-types
on tin: lotus, cedar, pond marigold.

Three things I'm sure of,
one of them's not you.

Walking in the midst of others,
one returns alone.

The blind crow will find you.
Rub your eyes; you'll both disappear.

Cousin to the dragonfly, the iris bloom
drops in on its stem for a visit.

Blessed be he who made coconuts, St. Theresa said.
They're certainly something to see.

If I'm going to be bald
let me be the eagle.

Dust on the grass. Now there's a smell
I'm used to. The rain refines it.

When a cat's halfway to being coyote,
a fox is what you get.

The wind called "the one that plucks the fowl"
leaves the trumpet swan unruffled.

Dewlap, lapwing, the near rhyme
of lost things the moon completes.

He opens his mouth and a bird flies in.
It shuts him up, all right.

Everything I know could fit
inside a sparrow's skeleton.

If this is your land, where are your stories?
the Elder asked in Tsimshian.

There's nothing smarter
than a river. Let's sit there for a while.

Pawprints on the grey slate near the pond.
A ghost cat sips the darkness.

My mother gave away lilacs by the armful.
Then we moved to a poorer place.

The public pool where I swam each morning?
They buried it beneath my feet.

There's a sadness I can't shake.
Old dog, don't come near me.

Tufts of hair between his toes,
the cat trails petals across the floor.

Three things blooming in our yard:
plum tree (pink and white), clematis, forsythia.

At the bottom of the pot, the skeleton of a mouse
who couldn't climb the glaze. His tail, too.

To wish you every happiness on your special day.
Soon I'll be the mother of my bones.

So the birds sound different here.
So the poplars and the wind. . . .

Monet paints "The Path Through the Irises."
It's the way I'm looking for.

The moon never disappears.
It just closes its one good eye.

The man who called the wolves
was shot by a fellow hunter.

There's danger in being
too good at what you do.

Take it to the left, the musicians say.
Then bring it home.

Break the line, my friend. The future's
three pennies, how they turn and fall.

Someone painted "Bird Love" on the birdhouse.
Simplicity without a trace of irony.

Where are your songs, your stories?
A list of things you cannot own.

Lilacs, especially.
Now there's a phrase I'll use.

A broom to sweep the doorway.
Words, these words to bring you home.

The Shape of the Journey. Boat or train?
Or your two good feet, in boots.

The otter drew the dog out to sea.
My friend thought they were playing.

A Vietnamese proverb says
Bamboo is my brother. And my love?

Eleven in our garden, mainly Golden;
they bend when they hear laughter.

Those hollows behind your ankles —
a place for wings? The sun won't let you.

I must admit I helped your hat get lost.
It looked so silly on your head.

If in truth you have a kind heart,
ask not. The why of wasps.

I am full of questions,
the where of you on what highway.

Ways to make the blood dance
when it leaves the body. Here's how not.

A rosary of rain clicks
between the wind's cold fingers.

Nightingale, sorrow, departing caravan
with horses. Panegyric to the rose.

The old one's poem has a sheen about it.
Unborn egg inside a hen.

Memorize the eye in everything.
Now the night sees only you.

Moon salt gathered from the sea:
fifteen years to learn its many uses.

Night. Suddenly beside me,
dark chest heaving, a woman on a horse.

Under the stars on the wooden deck
two dogs grin, their teeth too bright.

A peacock's tail sees technicolour:
rotting apples, arbutus, red tongue.

Around the fossil's rill of bones, the stains
that once were flesh. Remember that.

Stinking Rose: the other name for Garlic.
Give us a smile, the master said.

Birds break the dawn. Bang of wings
against the eastern window.

During drought, Sufis dance in every field,
twirling in brown robes and in grey.

The Pacific — not what I expected:
so large, so full of disregard.

Under the bridge with "Free Tibet" and "Bad Boyz,"
someone's written "I love your feet."

The simplest things / last. You must
climb the plum tree to see the blossom.

The dead gather: black flower, burnt book,
ruby head where the blood exploded.

Left out in the rain: what is ruined,
what's made better?

There's a woman dancing in the wind.
Her heart, a strange garment.

Skunks tap on hives, draw out the bees,
then eat them like popcorn.

Consider this: birds created before bats,
before us, but not before insects.

Too much going, nothing coming back;
the river never gaining ground.

There's poison in the egg that smells of almonds.
Green potatoes, nightcap, love letter.

It's midnight in my mother's belly.
Someone burns an effigy of stars.

Is anything more beautiful, more
useful than a wooden clothespin?

Night turns its wrists to smell
the winter jasmine.

The honey of the root, its dark harvest.
The parsnip's sweeter than the apple.

You say you're done with chopping wood.
Our fire will come from somewhere else.

Twenty-three years, the love of one good man:
The Green Sea of Heaven.

Prayed for rain. Got a dry rain instead.
Didn't know I had to ask for wet.

The changing and the changed —
the line, our bodies, your sweet tongue.

The earth spreads its cloths nubbed
and knotted. Tread softly on my dreams.

This slow and steady going,
a poor water sifts through silt.

Prepare a place for me. I built it out of
stone and wood, not knowing what he meant.

What of the wind's wordless singing?
The aspen signs whole alphabets of light.

Zuihitsu: follow the brush —
the bristle's rasp across my skin.

I change my name from *Storm*
to *Redtail*. Bones and wings.

Koi flash their copper coins, foretelling.
How much darkness makes a night?

All this talk from crows at 2 a.m.
I start over. Read the broken.

The pond's a hexagram whose lesson is
repeated: everything you lose comes round.

The space between the mouth and pen?
Too small to measure with the eye.

Ear to ear, you tell me there's no sea
inside me. Crows in the third place mean.

That old man climbing from the dry well —
look, his feet are wet!

Make a list of weeping trees: willow,
white birch, uncomely caragana.

Háfiz sat in a circle for forty days.
Did he become God's eye?

First line for the lake's love poem:
the long throat of the pickerel.

Walking the earth with you, my love,
one breath, one hour sacred to sorrow.

If loss had a language it would be water's.
We are mostly made of it.

Verbum salutis from the mouths of stars.
Go where you can hear the sky.

NOTES TO THE GHAZALS

The unattributed italicized quotations in ghazals 2, 7, 8, 11, 14, 19, 26 and 34 are from the *I Ching*. The sources of the other unidentified quotations or titles are listed below.

8   *Your feet's too big*, from the Fats Waller song.

12 *Here is your water and your watering place*, from Robert Frost's "Directive."

13 *No worse, there is none*, the opening phrase from one of Gerard Manly Hopkins's "dark sonnets."

19 *Díwán* is the title of the collected works of Háfiz.

22 *She said she'd marry me if I changed / my name to Moon and blew up the pipeline.* Overheard in a bar in Blue River, British Columbia.

30 *Lilacs especially*, from John Brady's *A Stone of the Heart*.

31 *The Shape of the Journey* is the title of Jim Harrison's selected poems.

36 *The simplest things / last*, from Charles Olson's "Maximus, to Himself."

38 *The Green Sea of Heaven* is a collection of Háfiz's ghazals, translated by Elizabeth T. Gray, Jr.

39 *Prepare a place for me* is a reworking of Jesus's words to his disciples in St. John 14:2

41 *Verbum salutis* is Latin for word of salvation.

Dreaming the Ghazal into Being

SOME BEAUTIFUL THING YOU HAVE MADE

If I ask questions, you'll show me
some beautiful thing you have made.[1]

I first came across the ghazal in 1978 in John Thompson's *Stilt Jack*, and part of my world changed forever. Those of you who know the book — which quickly became a classic among writers, passed by word of mouth and from hand to hand — will remember that after the poet's death, a friend sent the manuscript to Thompson's publisher and lover, Shirley Gibson, who took it to Anansi. For reasons that I hope will become obvious, I want to start my brief discussion of the ghazal with Thompson's last testament, one that his former mentor and teacher A.J.M. Smith called "so unique as to be beyond originality."

What we know of Thompson's life during his last few years — his self-destructiveness, his mental illness, his alcoholism — changes how we read the book.[2] We see his impending death in so many of the lines, from the startling, "Pigs fattened on boiled potatoes; horses mooning in hay; / in the woodshed he blew off his head with a shotgun," to the lyrically elegiac, "when I meet you again I'll be all light / all dark, all dark," to the seemingly innocent, "I pick over /

last night's food." For years many of Thompson's fans, reading autobiography into the images, believed he had shot himself with his hunting gun near New Brunswick's Tantramar Marshes. In reality, he died less dramatically but just as tragically from a lethal combination of whiskey and pills in his apartment in Sackville. His death at age 38 may have been accidental, but he had prepared for it for weeks, composing a will, leaving burial instructions, making various goodbyes to those he loved, and trusting his farewell manuscript to a poet friend for safekeeping. "At the very least, [he] put himself in death's way," wrote the editor of his collected poems, Peter Sanger.

The 38 ghazals in *Stilt Jack* (notice the number corresponds with his age) possess a remarkable, almost otherworldly power. Their posthumous publication and the tragic brevity of Thompson's life give them a fierce intensity. The poems resonate with what Lorca called *duende*, an artist's sense of the presence of death, its black baptismal water flowing through every moment of the creative act, whether it be the making of a song, a painting, or a poem. In such a state of awareness, the mind moves quickly, words get pared to the bone, familiar objects — a fish hook, a knife, a stove — seem created anew and have a glow about them. The form itself, no matter who the writer, opens the door to the cold breath of *duende* and invites it in. In his introduction to a collection of contemporary

54

ghazals, the editor Agha Shahid Ali gives us the etymology of the name itself and the origin of the grief that colours such a poem. The word *ghazal* (pronounced *guzzle*) comes from "the cry of the gazelle when it is cornered in a hunt and knows it will die."[3]

Thompson's ghazals possess this sense of urgency and darkness. The laconic, stripped-down diction simulates the lacunae in his writing life and eerily predicts the long silence that was to come. The last line of the sequence, hopeful and generous, removes the poet himself from the act of writing and leaves us with what his pain, love, and insight wrought in the dark company of his last few years: "Friends, these words for you."

No matter what his state when he wrote these words, no matter how difficult his life had become, Thompson was an exacting poet, crafting each phrase until it had the gleam of finely polished wood, the sharpness of a fish hook, the taste of salt, raw onions, and blood. But the poems offer something else to the reader and to the poets who follow in his shadow. Suddenly, with its publication in 1978, two years after his death, *Stilt Jack* introduced a new poetic form into the Canadian literary landscape.

Sometimes, if readers are lucky, in a certain writer's life form and content come together like two strangers who suddenly know they are about to experience a great and passionate love. Think of Whitman taking into his huge lungs and generous heart the music of the King James Version of the Bible and transforming it into his own long-legged, muscular line. Think of Dante inventing *terza rima*, that three-line stanza that pulls us inexorably through *The Divine Comedy*, the linked rhyme of the middle lines hooking together like the cars of a ghost train descending deeper into the inferno and then ascending the luminous tracks into paradise. Or consider the stars' realignment when John Berryman settled on three six-line stanzas for his greatest achievement, his over one hundred "dream songs." The eighteen lines of each song hold on to the intensity of the sonnet, yet the extra four lines give him enough room to wander between his alter-egos and to radically shift the tone and diction within each small piece.

Thompson, of course, didn't invent the ghazal. It is an ancient Persian lyric from the eighth century. He probably discovered it, not in its original source, but in the work of his friend Jim Harrison, whom he met as a student at the University of Michigan and who used the form in *Outlyer and Ghazals*, published in 1971.[4] In his introduction to Thompson's collected poems, Peter Sanger tells us that Harrison's ghazals (inspired by a series by Adrienne Rich) had a great influence on Thompson and that he circulated them among students in his writing classes at Mount Allison. I don't think it goes too far to say, however, that

Thompson reinvented the form in English for *our* country. It is his book, unique for its time, that pointed Phyllis Webb and Patrick Lane — to name two of our most prominent poets — in the direction of the ghazal. Her *Water and Light: Ghazals and Anti Ghazals* was first published in 1982 and Patrick Lane's *A Linen Crow, A Caftan Magpie* in 1984. Both speak of *Stilt Jack's* influence and allude to it in their lines. Webb does so most directly, invoking his name in her opening couplet: "I semaphore for help (calling stone-dead John Thompson)."

In the early nineties when free verse began to budge a little and allow room for a revived interest in traditional poetry, writers in Canada would have stumbled upon the ghazal as they did upon the pantoum and glosa. Thompson, however, got us there fifteen years earlier. He established a standard, a challenge. And his nimble side-stepping of its restrictions has given the go-ahead to writers here to push the edges of this traditional form in their own English versions. Thompson's ghazals are what Shakespeare's sonnets must have been to his contemporaries — notes of excellence others aspire to, all of us giving a nod in Thompson's direction whenever we venture up that path, calling on his help.

HOW SMALL A POEM CAN BE

I know how small a poem can be:
the point on a fish hook;

Any form with such a long history and established
conventions creates complexities that writers outside
of the founding culture cannot possibly understand
or explain. The Persian mystics Rumi (1207-73) and
Háfiz-i Shírází (1325-1389) were undisputed masters
of the classical ghazal in Persian, and four centuries
later, Ghalib (1797-1869) of the form in Urdu. I have
read these poets only in English versions. Recalling
Frost's adage that poetry is what gets lost in transla-
tion, I'm painfully aware that I'm missing a lot, espe-
cially the music of Persian and Urdu. The same holds
true for my understanding of the traditional form. Not
being an Arabic scholar, I have to trust the research
and knowledge of others and my study of the ghazal
in English to come anywhere close to catching a
glimpse of its character.

The *Princeton Encyclopedia of Poetry and Poetics* is al-
ways a good place to start. In a relatively short entry,
it defines the ghazal as a lyric in Eastern literature from
the eighth century onward, "whose theme is gener-
ally love and wine, often mystically understood."[5] It

"varies in length from 5 to 12 couplets all upon the same rhyme. The poet signs his name in the final couplet" (323). A further explanation of the form's stringency is offered by Agha Shahid Ali in his introduction to *Ravishing Disunity, Real Ghazals in English*. The word "real" will give you an idea of the polemical tone of his remarks — he believes an unrhymed ghazal is a contradiction in terms — but his definition of the conventional form is useful. So is the one offered in the introduction to Háfiz's *The Green Sea of Heaven*, translated by Elizabeth T. Gray, and in John Thompson's and Jim Harrison's brief prefaces to their two collections. It is also worth looking at Aijaz Ahmad's succinct description in his foreword to *Ghazals of Ghalib*. To sum up what they and others have to say, here is a simplified version of the basic characteristics of the ghazal:

1. The ghazal is made up of couplets (called *shers*), a minimum of five, a maximum of twelve though many have been longer.

2. The couplets must be closed. That is, there is no enjambment between them. Each self-contained distich has been compared to the pearl on a necklace and a world within a larger world; it possesses its own sense of conclusiveness and intrinsic beauty. Of course if the couplets run together, the effect of a mini-poem within

a poem will vanish, and the reader will encounter a different musical movement, progression, and tenor.

I don't know how successful any of my attempts in this form have been, but I do know that the decision you make about the kind of couplet you are going to use at the outset influences everything that follows. In my previous attempts at ghazals, I allowed myself to elide couplets; in the sequence that precedes these notes I did not. One kind of ghazal isn't superior to the other, but I found the writing processes and the results radically dissimilar. There was an ease, a roominess to writing run-on couplets (something Thompson occasionally allows himself) that disappeared when they had to be autonomous and end-stopped. The enforced economy of two stand-alone lines, rather than the fluid run-on of four or six spilling over the spaces between stanzas, puts tremendous pressure on the syntax, diction, and images. A different kind of poetry animal comes into being, mammalian like the other but as similar as a horse is to a langur. The challenge in writing free-standing couplets is to avoid a flat, predictable regularity even though the length of the units is predetermined and immutable. You have to try to vary the music and word-order within a confined, unelastic space. And you have to be willing to give up anything that resembles narrative. Story is sacrificed for suggestion, implication, allusion.

3. The couplets are linked by a mono-rhyme (*qafia*) that precedes a refrain (*radif*). The refrain may be either a word or a phrase. Here's an example:

> In days of darkness will anything please you
>   except the snow?
> After the blizzard the sky leaves no clues except
>   the snow.

In the first *sher*, the refrain must conclude both lines. In the couplets that follow, the refrain concludes the second line only. In other words, all of the couplets must end with "except the snow" and the rhyme sound, in this case the long "u" in the opening line, must fall immediately before that phrase. Below, I follow the established pattern in a second *sher* with the inclusion of the *radif* and the *qafia* "beauty":

> Orange pekoe, tea rose, Darjeeling. What's
>   wrong with this list?
> Nothing increases the osier's beauty except the
>   snow.

When the poems were recited or sung, as they were traditionally, the audience would wait for the second line to near its end, then join in with the refrain, creating a response/reply dialectic between the poet and his listeners. Perhaps the poet gave a signal with a gesture or a shift in the tone of his voice. That buildup of expectation followed by fulfillment must have been extraordinarily pleasing to the thousands of poetry lovers who gathered to hear their favourite ghazal master. They became part of the writing of the poem, or at least part of its becoming alive again in the mouth and the ear.

The contemporary practitioners of ghazals whom I refer to here have avoided using the *radif* and *qafia*. So have my favourite translators of Ghalib, Rumi and Háfiz. When the rhymes and refrains come so close together with just one relief-line in between, it's difficult to avoid monotony. I felt a predictability in the majority of the poems in Agha Shahid Ali's recent anthology of ghazals, all of which use a rhyme and a refrain as outlined above. He makes an impassioned and cranky argument for following these strictures of the orthodox scheme, but even the good writers he includes seem shackled, and the flight feathers of swift-moving couplets get clipped.

English is famously rhyme-poor, many words having only one mate and several having none. Harrison, Rich, Thompson, Webb, and Lane wrote unrhymed, refrainless ghazals of remarkable delicacy and power. Urdu writer Aijaz Ahmad supports this modern tendency away from terminal rhyme in his introductory comments to his collection of Ghalib translations: "Inner rhymes, allusions, verbal associations, wit, and

62

imagistic relations can quite adequately take over the functions performed by the end-rhymes in the original Urdu" (xix).

4. Each line must be of the same length and meter. In Urdu and Persian, writers counted syllables like the Japanese haiku and tanka poets. Because English is stress-based, the syllabic system, like rhyme, doesn't complement the character of the language as it does the mother-tongues of the ghazal's origin. Even when the mathematics of syllables are meticulously controlled, in English we tend to hear the rise and fall of accented and unaccented sounds rather than the number of syllables. Thus this rule often gets broken or at least loosened up.

5. The final couplet usually includes the poet's name. This signature couplet is called *makhta*. Here's an example from Háfiz, translated by Elizabeth Gray, Jr:

Háfiz, place your head on the threshold of
    submission,
for if you argue, fate will argue back.

And one from Ghalib, translated by Robert Bly:

I know that heaven doesn't exist, but the idea
Is one of Ghalib's favorite fantasies.

6. By the tenth century when ghazals became conventionalized, along with the common theme of love and wine, the Persian courts called for the appearance of stock images such as roses, nightingales, deserts, and departing caravans. The test of a poet's mettle was his ability to use the familiar images in innovative ways.

7. Finally, and most important to our discussion, the order of the couplets is "clandestine," to use Thompson's word. There is no obvious relation between one and the other, no clear chronology. This means the couplets are self-sufficient and independent enough to be moved around like pearls on a necklace, even a few deleted, without changing the meaning or effect. To the Western mind raised on the well-made, integrated poem that introduces a theme or subject and moves progressively towards a resolution, this is perhaps the most difficult quality to understand, and the most alluring. Sometimes the poems don't seem to be going anywhere, even towards their own indefinite conclusions; often the ideas and images seem unrelated. As readers we are asked to do a lot of the work. The form demands trust as we look through the glass darkly to see or intuit the hidden harmony that is there.

My introduction of the ghazal to students over the past fifteen years has usually met with puzzlement, followed by resistance and frustration, and finally, for some, delight. You can hear that delight in Shannon Bailey's ghazals, which started out as part of a directed study and ended up as an award-winning chapbook: "So you call me a hermit crab. / I sink down into the bathwater, hoping // I won't make any more glib promises. / (I'm heading wet to the mood I was in.)"[6]

I'LL LEARN BY GOING WHERE I HAVE TO GO

I'll learn by going:
Sleave-silk flies; the kindly ones.

Of these simplified "rules" of the form, Thompson holds fast to only a few — he wrote in couplets, and he stayed within the magical length of between five and twelve.[7] Though many of his couplets meet the requirement of being end-stopped, he allowed enough of them to slip and slide between one another to make a noticeable break in the pattern. What he avoids altogether is the refrain, the rhyme, the strict meter and regular line length, and he includes his "own strange name" in only one concluding couplet. But what he does adhere to, and what makes *Stilt Jack* a series of ghazals rather than a series of free-verse lyrics, is how the couplets leap, one to the other.

Unlike sonnets, for instance, or the majority of free-verse lyrics and narratives written in this century, the ghazal is daringly nonlinear. The connection between couplets (except when they run together) is subliminal, subtle, often produced by sound rather than meaning. You can see how this would appeal to contemporary poets and our distrust of the ordered universe and the tock / tock of the logic-metronome. The poets Thompson admired who come closest to this alluring disorder, this rattling of syntactical bones in their own work (although, to my knowledge, they didn't write ghazals) are Berryman and Roethke. You can sense a gazelle-like presence gazing from the shadows cast by such lines as "Arch my back, pretty-bones, I'm dead at both ends. / Softly, softly, you'll wake the clams" (from Roethke's "Praise to the End!") and " And the tranquil hills, & gin, look like a drag / and somehow a dog / has taken itself and its tail considerably away. . . ." (from number 14 in Berryman's "77 Dream Songs").[8]

More than most other forms, including free verse, the ghazal allows the poet to hold a mirror up to the nimble, discursive movements of the mind (it's heading wet to the mood it's in). One flash of thought sparks on the heels of another. Intuition, slips of the tongue, and fiery imagination forge fast associations that flare like phosphorous in the dark. The form has the spontaneity of a dance; as Jim Harrison says, it is "faithful only to its own music." The logic is there, but it's a different kind than we're used to. One of the most useful analogies I've come across to illustrate the way the couplets relate to one another is the comparison of the poem to the surface of a pool. Two or three themes are dropped into the water like stones creating circles of images that move outward, touch, and overlap. Their intersection weaves a complicated expanding pattern of meaning and resonance, but the pattern is composed of the ripples from the individual stones.

From his short preface to *Stilt Jack*, here are Thompson's own words on this matter: "The link between couplets (five to a poem) is a matter of tone, nuance: the poem has no palpable intention on us. It breaks, has to be listened to as song: its order is clandestine." He goes on to say, "The ghazal allows the imagination to move by its own nature: discovering an alien design, illogical and without sense — a chart of the disorderly, against false reason and the tacking together of poor narratives."

It is this "alien design," this multi-faceted disorder, that most intrigues contemporary writers and that says the most about the essence of the form. It brings out a poet's magpie mind; it encourages the audacious and saucy. Daring as a thief, the poet steals the bright particulars wherever he or she finds them and puts them in the poem's many-storied, twiggy nest. For such a brief poem, it's capacious. There's room for everything: allusions to other poets, an old stove, meditations on death, quotations, the horns of a snail. The form challenges our notions of what can be brought together and held. With a delightful inclusiveness, Háfiz used imagery from all over his psychic map, from Islamic law and alchemy to the flora and fauna of his beautiful city. The ghazal invites everyone and everything through the gates of its walled garden.

It is a poem of paradoxes, of strange couplings, balances, unusual metonymies, apostrophes, fragments, and startling shifts of tone. The poet can be sad, ironic, playful, meditative, even silly, all within ten to twenty-four lines. The uncommon is at home in the ghazal — from strange pairings of images to varieties of punctuation and kinds of sentences. You'll see more imperatives, exclamations, and questions than you do in most other lyrics, all of them nudging the declarative out of its prominent place. The lines will be studded with exclamation marks, colons, and dashes — suggesting a state of excitement, sparks flying from something new being made. Ghalib exclaims, "Fire runs from my burning eyes, Asad! / I light up the soil and the dead leaves in my garden" (translated by Mark Strand).

A friend who has been working on a ghazal sequence for the last few years told me that she'd rarely written about birds in her other poems, but her ghazals are full of them. It is a winged form, a singing form, one that defies gravity with its lightness yet is capable of mystical weight. Its nearest relative, in terms of the impression it makes, is the haiku. There is the same sense of *now* in the images, the same sense of presence, of affirming that this is *this* (to repeat an insight from Robert Hass) rather than this is *that*. As in haiku, the most resonant of the couplets gives you the feeling that something wild or singular has just walked through. The double lines are the tracks this charisma leaves.

Like the haiku's three lines, many of the ghazal's couplets are framed by a deep silence, the unsaid surrounding the few words that have broken through. Yet unlike the haiku's silence and its companionable stillness, the couplet's closure is not allowed to last, for one seemingly complete pair of lines is followed by another tugging it forward until the inconclusive finale. Each couplet's end-stop is a stop on ice. Like a Noh actor, the ghazal stanza seems to move and stand still at the same time. This combination of pause and movement, of muteness and utterance, is one of the form's most fascinating paradoxes. We can learn something about it from Rumi. When he was asked to explain why he *talked* so much about silence, he replied, "The radiant one inside me has never said a word."

Ghazals have been enriched by mysticism since the twelfth and thirteenth centuries when Sufi writers like Rumi and Háfiz used the form to forge their personal and ecstatic union with God, who was often conflated with their beloved.[9] The lack of distinction between genders in Persian and Urdu pronouns and their use of lower rather than upper case to refer to the deity make this fusion possible. The closest English can come to the same ambiguity is through the use of "you," which can be male or female, human or god. And sometimes we can get away with "it," what Charles Simic calls the most interesting word in our language. Whatever pronoun is used, traces of mysticism remain in ghazal compositions. Couplets like Thompson's "Loaves of bread remembered: / eat salt and tell the truth" become gnomic utterances, the commonplace turning into the iconic. And many of the imperatives and axioms that find their home in ghazals achieve the force of wisdom lines.

You'll come across more of these than you're used to in contemporary poems, but I find them palatable because more often than not, they remain grounded in the world of everyday things and in the senses, particularly smell and taste. The best ones have a pleasing lightness of touch and sometimes humour. Here's one from Rumi: "Don't be a cat toying with a mouse. / Go after the love lion." As well, because of the ambiguity of the pronoun "you," including the one addressed in imperatives like Rumi's, we're never sure if the advice is for the reader, the beloved, or the poet himself. He may be talking out loud, operating as his own teacher, directing his soul and heart to more luminous ways of being as he dervishly whirls and writes his way into enlightenment.

In the poems I return to, there's also a refreshing lack of the ecclesiastic along with a love of ambiguity. A poet capable of living with contradictions, of saying this *and* that rather than this *or* that, can pass on his insights and guidance to me any time.[10] Thompson writes, "If I give everything away / it's because I want to take everything," and "I love to watch the trout rising / as I fall, fall." In ghazals, paradoxes show up like tricksters, who save everyone from sureties and self-importance and get them up to dance before the music stops.

Thompson uses one of Roethke's lines from the villanelle "The Waking" as a subtle refrain in *Stilt Jack*: "I learn by going where I have to go." That line says a lot about how a ghazal gets written. In a state that resembles the "drunken and amatory" (Thompson's phrase), the poet lets one image travel into another, with no traffic cop controlling what gets on the road — Mercedes, pick-up truck, horse and buggy, Pegasus — and no red or yellow lights. The phenomenological collides with the metaphysical, the daily with the eternal, the high with the low. There are the gazelle's death cry and phrases that seem to fall from some holy text, but there are also lines from popular songs, drunken self-pity, amusing challenges to Yeats. What you get

71

and how you compose is what Robert Bly calls for in his rallying call for "leaping poetry." Poets look for the inner life of familiar objects — the breath inside the stone — and associate fast. The pedestrian mind gets left behind as the poet sinks in darkness and strides through stars. That's when the voice of the holy and the telluric can be heard. No wonder the ghazal holds such an attraction, such charm. It is a form for lovers and lunatics.

In ghazal XXV, Thompson writes: "If I ask questions, you'll show me / some beautiful thing you have made." It is the questions his last words engender that have led Canadian poets like Webb and Lane to make a beautiful thing in the form he brought to our attention, one so suited to the delight, melancholy, and contradictions of our disordered age. Their ghazals continue the conversation Thompson started in our country. My friends, with humility, I add these words for you.

1 The epigraphs after each subtitle are from John Thompson's *Stilt Jack* (Toronto: Anansi, 1978).

2 For an account of Thompson's difficult behaviour the last few years of his life, refer to Jim Polk's introduction to the poet's collected, *I Dream Myself Into Being* (Toronto: Anansi, 1991).

3 There's an irony to this pronunciation: you can't help but think of its meaning in English: "to drink greedily or immoderately." Thompson used this pun in conversations with friends about what he was working on. For years, I deliberately mispronounced the word because I prefer the connotations of grace and beauty that *gazelle* brings with its sound.

4 There's no doubt that Thompson would have sought out the Urdu and Persian masters of the form after his reading of Harrison. He was a scholar, after all, receiving his PhD in Comparative Literature from Michigan University, his thesis a translation of René Char, whose poems also had an influence on Thompson's ghazal writing.

5 One of Ghalib's translators, Sunil Dutta, makes an amusing distinction between the use of the words *wine* and *tavern* by Ghalib and by Sufi poets like Rumi. When the latter use them they mean the state of the soul and religious ecstasy. "When Ghalib uses these words, he means wine and taverns" (64).

6 Shannon Bailey's series of ghazals, "Landscape of Devotion," was the Canadian winner of Mother Tongue's Poetry Chapbook Competition in 1995, judged by Phyllis Webb, Brian Brett, and Daphne Marlatt.

7 Phyllis Webb also sticks to the traditional number, but in *A Linen Crow, A Caftan Magpie,* Patrick Lane breaks the rule and uses only four. Unlike the couplets of Thompson and Webb, all of his are end-stopped. When asked why he used one fewer than the prescribed, Lane said that it was the only way he was able to stop himself from drifting into a hint of narrative and from stitching together the couplets in any other way.

8 I'd like to suggest that Roethke and Berryman are progenitors of the ghazal in English, even though they didn't write in that form. Their syntactical surprises and metaphoric leaps made their admirers, including poets like Thompson, open to accepting such shifts and wanting more.

9 The joyous praise of the beloved (divine or human) permeates the couplets in Rumi's and Háfiz's ghazals. Although there are amazing variations in metaphor and tone, from *sher* to *sher* these poets thread the ecstatic music of his beatific presence. It ties the couplets together.

10 Ghalib is famous for defining himself as a *half*-Muslim. When asked how that could be, he replied. "Sir, I don't eat pork, but I do drink wine."

Ali, Agha Shahid. "Ghazal: The Charms of a Considered Disunity." *The Practice of Poetry: Writing Exercises from Poets Who Teach*. Edited by Chase Twitchell and Robin Behn. New York: Harper Perennial, 1992.
_____ (ed.). *Ravishing Disunities, Real Ghazals in English*. Hanover: Wesleyan University Press, 2000.

Bailey, Shannon. *Landscape of Devotion*. Saltspring Island: Mother Tongue Press, 1995.

Bly, Robert. *Leaping Poetry*. Boston: Beacon Press, 1975.

Crozier, Lorna. *Eye Witness*. Victoria: Reference West, 1993.
_____ "If I Call Stones Blue (Ghazal Variations for the Spring Equinox)." *Everything Arrives at the Light*. Toronto: McClelland & Stewart, 1995.
_____ *The Transparency of Grief*. Salt Spring Island: Mother Tongue Press, 1996.

Ghalib. *Ghazals of Ghalib, Versions from the Urdu*. Edited by Aijaz Ahmad. Translated by W. S. Merwin, Adrienne Rich, William Stafford, David Ray, Thomas Fitzsimmons, Mark Strand, and William Hunt. New York: Oxford University Press, 1994
_____ *Ghazals of Ghalib. Ghazals of Ghalib*. Translated by Shasha Newborn. Santa Barbara: Bandana Books, 2000.
_____ *The Lightning Should Have Fallen on Ghalib*. Translated by Robert Bly and Sunil Dutta). Hopewell, NJ: Ecco, 1999.

Háfiz. *The Green Sea of Heaven*. Translated by Elizabeth T. Gray. Introduction by Daryush Shayegan. Ashland, OR: White Cloud Press, 1995.

Harrison, Jim. *The Shape of the Journey*. Port Townsend: Copper Canyon Press, 1998.

Lane, Patrick. *A Linen Crow, A Caftan Magpie*. Saskatoon: Thistledown, 1984.

Rich, Adrienne. *Leaflets*. New York: Norton, 1978.
_____ *Facts of a Doorframe*. New York: Norton, 1984.

Rumi. *The Essential Rumi*. Translated by Coleman Barks. San Franciso: HaperSanFrancisco, 1995.
_____ *The Soul of Rumi*. Translated by Coleman Barks. San Francisco: HarperSanFrancisco, 2001.

Thompson, John. *At the Edge of the Chopping There are No Secrets*. Toronto: Anansi, 1973.
_____ *I Dream Myself Into Being: Collected Poems*. Toronto: Anansi, 1991.
_____*John Thompson: Collected Poems & Translations*. Edited by Peter Sanger). Fredericton: Goose Lane, 1995.
_____ *Stilt Jack*. Toronto: Anansi, 1978.

Webb, Phyllis. *Water and Light, Ghazals and Anti-Ghazals*. Toronto: Coach House, 1983.

ALSO BY LORNA CROZIER

Inside Is the Sky · 1976

Crow's Black Joy · 1979

Humans and Other Beasts · 1980

No Longer Two People (with Patrick Lane) · 1981

The Weather · 1983

The Garden Going On Without Us · 1985

Angels of Flesh, Angels of Silence · 1988

Inventing the Hawk · 1992

Everything Arrives at the Light · 1995

A Saving Grace: The Collected Poems of Mrs. Bentley · 1996

What the Living Won't Let Go · 1999

Apocrypha of Light · 2002

PHOTO BY BRIAN BRETT

Lorna Crozier is the author of twelve volumes of poetry, including the Governor General's Award winning *Inventing the Hawk; The Collected Poems of Mrs. Bentley*, inspired by Sinclair Ross's classic *As for Me and My House*; and *What the Living Won't Let Go*, winner of the Dorothy Livesay Poetry Prize. Born in Swift Current, Saskatchewan, she teaches creative writing at the University of Victoria and gives writing workshops around the country.

Bones in Their Wings is set in Weiss BT, a
typeface originally designed by the
German calligrapher Emil Rudolf
Weiss (1875–1942), the roman in
1924, the italic in 1926. This digital
version is published by Bitstream.

The cover design is based on tile work
from a Persian sanctuary, circa 1428.

This book was designed and typeset
by Donald Ward.

Edited by Paul Wilson.